Copyright© 2009 Simple Truths, LLC

Published by SimpleTruths, LLC
1952 McDowell Road
Naperville, Illinois 60563

Design: Lynn Harker, Simple Truths, Illinois
Edited by: Stephanie Trannel

Simple Truths is a registered trademark.
Printed and bound in the United States of America

ISBN 978-1-60810-033-0

800-900-3427
www.simpletruths.com

03 WOZ 10

TWICE AS MUCH IN HALF THE TIME

Amy Jones

Secrets to Simplifying Your Life

Table of Contents

Introduction

{ *Who WOULDN'T want to be able to do twice as much in half the time?* }

I have good news for you. It ***can*** be done. You have already made a good start just by opening the first page of this book. By the time you reach the final page, you should be ready to go out and do twice *(and maybe even three times!)* as much as before.

√ *So don't waste any more time ...*
GET STARTED!

Foreword

It is such a pleasure to write this foreword for my friend Amy Jones. Amy is one of the many, many people I have encouraged over the years to write a book, and one of the few I am aware of who have actually taken that advice *(and lived to tell about it!)*.

It has been rewarding to watch Amy develop her talents and skills over the past several years. She shared her story for the first time with us at Ziglar at our Monday morning staff devotional meeting. It was obvious even then that she had the talent and skills necessary to deliver her message with heart, with a compassion that would touch those in her audiences in a very meaningful way.

Amy came to us with considerable experience in the field of professional selling. What she didn't realize at the time was that when she combined her selling skills with her inimitable story-telling talent, she could have a positive influence on the lives of many others—a mission that has since become her passion.

One of the topics Amy teaches is time management. She gives her presentations with enthusiasm and with a heart for the people she hopes and believes her own experiences can serve. She writes that

 way, too. I believe that as you read Amy's book you will be informed, educated, encouraged, uplifted and strengthened in your own commitment to take control of the mere 24 hours you have every day to accomplish your objectives. I also believe you will be entertained by her unique and personal style of writing, which mirrors her outstanding stage presence. This book offers you, the reader, the pleasant experience of delving into a subject that can literally change your life as you enjoy reading how Amy Jones has become, and continues to be, an authority on the subject of making every moment of your life count—for you and for others.

Zig Ziglar

Mind Your Own Busy-ness

> *The phone is RINGING ... the meeting's in ten minutes ... that deadline was YESTERDAY ... my in-box is FULL.*
>
> # I'VE RUN OUT OF TIME!

Have you ever had a day like this? Are you thinking, "EVERY *day is like this*"? We live in a fast-paced, hurry-up, get-the-job-done world. It seems that the word "busy" is the buzz word of the 21st century.

Think about it. You run into a friend you haven't seen in awhile and ask, "How have you been?" You're likely to get this response: "I've been so busy." Perhaps you'll pass a co-worker in the hallway and ask, "How's it going?" He will probably shake his head and say, "Just too busy." The people around us are constantly trying to find time, add time, save time, or make more time. How can this be done without doubling the days in the week or the hours in the day? Are there ways we can learn to run our lives more effectively and efficiently to get more done in less time?

 Are there ways we can learn to do twice as much in half the time? **THERE ARE!**

Back to the Basics

{ WHAT DOES IT MEAN TO MANAGE YOUR TIME (and life) BETTER? }

Simply put, it means to live your life in such a way that you are able to accomplish more, so that at the end of each day you can realize measurable results and enjoy a sense of fulfillment. This often involves learning to do things differently so that the outcomes are more efficient and effective (and even less time-consuming) than before. After reading from countless resources and speaking to over half a million people on the subject of time management, I have come up with a simple truth. Learning to manage your life and your time isn't rocket science. **Anyone can do it!** In fact, it is often the simple things you can do that will make profound differences. Sometimes you even have to go backward in order to go forward; so let's go back-to-basics with this example.

First, grab a pencil and paper. Think back to the time you started school, all the way back to kindergarten. One of the first things you learned was how to identify shapes. Next you learned to draw them. On that sheet of paper I want you to do something very simple. Draw one triangle. That was simple, wasn't it? Now, draw as many triangles as you can in twenty seconds. Stop. Count how many you were able to draw. Write down that number. Do you think there might be another way to complete this activity and draw more in less time?

Start at one side of the paper and draw connected Ws all the way across the page. Now put a line across the top and the bottom. See how many you can draw in twenty seconds using this method. Wow, that creates a lot of triangles! In only a few seconds you have learned to do this activity more efficiently and effectively in a much shorter amount of time. A seemingly insignificant change can make a significant difference in what can be accomplished in a given amount of time. In fact, you most likely made up to four or five times as many triangles the second time around.

What if you could do four or five times your sales volume by making a simple change? Or what if you could get *four or five times as much done each day* by making a simple change? Would that work for you?

If so, always be on the **lookout for "new" ways** to do "old" things, and keep your mind open to using alternative methods and plans of action. This book is filled with simple things that can make a profound difference. *Are you ready to learn some new ways to manage your life and your time even better?*

THEN LET'S GET STARTED!

> You can learn new things at any time in your life if you're willing to be a beginner.
> If you actually learn to like being a beginner, the whole world opens up to you.
>
> Barbara Sher

Becoming Number 1

Sometimes life seems to be a numbers game.

√ HOW LARGE? ... HOW MUCH? ... HOW FAST?

Well, I have a really big number for you ... and it will make your day. In fact, it IS your day. That number is 86,400 ... and it's all yours!

You can use it, you can spend it, you can invest it, you can waste it, and you can even share it; but you can't save it, because tomorrow it will be completely gone. You see, 86,400 is the exact number of seconds you have each day—86,400 seconds that are yours to use or yours to lose. That number makes it sound like a huge amount of time, but how often do you find yourself saying, "If only I had just a little more time"?

Do we really need more time, or do we simply need to use our time more wisely? Not a single person has more time in any 24-hour day than you have—not the CEO of the world's largest corporation, not the president of the United States, not the parent of ten children— not even Bill Gates. Time is one area where we are all on an even playing field.

{ *Let's see how you can use time to become Number 1 in whatever you do!* }

An Equation for Effective Life Management

Large numbers ... small numbers ... all can be manipulated with mathematical equations. How can this help us in managing our time, in learning how to do twice as much in half the time?

{
Let's start with what I call ...

"TIME MANAGEMENT MATHEMATICS"
}

It goes like this: Subtracting $(-)$, Adding $(+)$, Multiplying (X), and Dividing $(/)$ Equals $(=)$ Successful Management of Life and Time.

$\sqrt{}$ When you start putting this equation into practice, amazingly you will find the answer to how you can do more in less time.

SUBTRACTING

Clutter

> { **SUBTRACTING?** WHY would you need to begin by subtracting? In order to ADD any time to your life you must first begin by **SUBTRACTING** the "stuff" in your life that steals your time. }

SUBTRACTING (—) PHYSICALLY:

Think about it: much of the time that we consider lost is actually stolen by the stuff in our lives—stuff we have to care for, look for, clean up, organize, or keep up with. I know it's true, for I am a genuine, self-professed, recovering "stuff-a-holic." I have even created an acronym to identify the stuff when it invades my own life. Superfluous Trivial Unnecessary Frivolous Fillers. Do you, by any chance, have that kind of STUFF in your own life?

Back in my "stuff-a-holic" days you could find massive amounts of stuff just about anywhere you found me. Back then I had a house that I loved and a job that I loved, and a three-hour round trip commute each day between those two places. Instead of worrying about misplacing, forgetting, or leaving behind something I might really need,

I just carried everything I needed from work or home in the car. My car was literally stuffed with stuff! It was one of those cars that you walk by in the parking lot and look inside and think, "I wonder if someone lives in that car?" Each weekend I usually spent over an hour cleaning out and "re-stuffing" my car.

Finally there came a day of reckoning with my stuff. On that day in May of 1995, the Dallas/ Fort Worth Metroplex was hit by the most devastating hailstorm in United States history, causing widespread damage and loss of lives. Further devastation was brought on by the accompanying violent thunderstorms. As the storms worsened, I found myself in the midst of that torrential downpour on a dark, unfamiliar residential street. I was no longer able to see the road ahead and did not even realize that I was crossing over a low-water bridge. Before it even registered with me, my car stalled in the flooding water. When the engine would not restart and I felt the car move, my first thought was, "I need to grab my important 'stuff' and get out of this car." Hastily I grabbed a few items and reached for the door. It wouldn't budge. In a moment of panic I began beating on the car window. Gaining control of myself, I realized I needed to push the button for the automatic window to open, hoping and praying that the electrical system had not yet shorted out in the flood.

 As the window opened, water immediately rushed into the car, but it wasn't the rain coming in. It was the rising floodwaters, which were swirling around my car. Within a few moments the water level came up to my chest. I knew within seconds the car *(with me in it)* would be under water. My life flashed before my eyes as I thought, "I can't save my stuff … I have to save my life!" I climbed out through the window, struggled to reach the car roof, and screamed at the top of my lungs. Just as the force of the undercurrent pulled me down, I reached out and grabbed at the fence that ran along the side of the bridge and held on with all my might. Someone inside a nearby house heard my cries and called 911. By forming a human chain with arms locked together, my rescuers withstood the rushing water and brought me to safety.

I stood in the pouring rain and watched as all that stuff that seemed so important was ruined or swept away by the flood waters. After the ordeal was over I realized that my belongings, both inside the car and in the trunk (which had been filled to capacity), were not that important after all. I didn't even replace ten percent of what had been in my car! *And to think ... I almost drowned in my own stuff!*

Years later, I recalled that terrifying night and how I had almost drowned in my own stuff. Do you ever feel like that? You may not have had a life-threatening experience, but aren't there days when you feel like you are drowning in your own stuff?

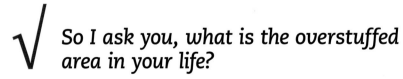 *So I ask you, what is the overstuffed area in your life?*

It may not be your car, but perhaps it is your office, work station, or closet ... or all of the above! How much time is wasted caring for, cleaning, organizing, or searching for all that stuff that clutters your environment?

The ability to simplify means to eliminate the unnecessary so that the necessary may speak.

Hans Hofmann

SUBTRACTING (—) MENTALLY:

Now is the time to start subtracting! So far we have considered the tangible stuff. But what about the intangible, *the stuff we can't see—worry, anxiety, unanswered questions, the everyday stresses—* that too often fills our hearts and heads? The stuff that infiltrates our minds to the point that we spend countless hours just thinking and worrying about it. None of this impacts the outcome.

But sometimes the intangible stuff consumes even more of our time than the tangible.

About five years ago my identity was stolen. I still can't figure out how it happened. My wallet wasn't missing. I did not lose my drivers license or credit cards. In fact, I did not lose anything—except my identity. Numerous credit cards were opened and maxed out in my name, two cell phone accounts were created, thousands of dollars were taken from my checking account, and the thief even used my savings account to pay off a credit card he had in collections! After making these startling discoveries, I spent the next three days dealing with the situation: checking my credit, calling credit bureaus, filing

a police report, canceling accounts, writing letters and getting them notarized, talking to cell phone providers … the list went on and on. It totally consumed three days of my time … but I had no choice. I did what I had to do to take control of the situation.

But then in the following days *(after I had done everything I could possibly do to correct the problem)* I could not mentally let go. I found myself worrying about the situation instead of catching up on my work. All I could think about was, "How did this happen?" My mind kept reeling with questions: "Who could have done this? How did they do it? Where are they? Since they know who I am and everything about me, are they going to try to assume my identity?" Such questions and concerns completely consumed my thoughts for several days before I realized that my thoughts *(the intangible stuff)* were stealing even more time from me. I needed to take my own advice and eliminate this mental stuff from my life. So I focused on the fact I had done everything in my power to deal with the situation and could do nothing else. It was the only way I was going to prevent myself from continuing to be a victim of an identity thief.

Please note that there is a big difference between needless worry and genuine concern. When you, by your own actions, can effectively change a situation, it is quite appropriate to have a certain level of concern over the outcome. However, when you continue to worry about something in your life over which you have no control, that worry quickly becomes the *stuff* that steals your time.

NOW is the time to begin **subtracting the stuff** in your life, whether it's tangible or intangible.

{
Employ
"SUBTRACTION ACTION"
on a daily basis and you will find yourself free to be more productive.
}

There are two
kinds of worries –
those you CAN do something
about and those you CAN'T.
Don't spend any
time on the latter.

Duke Ellington

ADDING

The "Plus" Factors

Now that we have subtracted, let's do the reverse process. Let's add. I like to call this step

"ADDING THE POSITIVE Ps."

There are four additions you can make that will change your life:

√ *Programs,*
Purpose,
Planning, and
Priorities.

ADD (+) PROGRAMS:

I am passionate about ***adding life-enhancing programs***—programs to advance your career, to further your education, to help you become more efficient and effective—so you can ultimately do more in less time. Go back to school, attend a seminar, or as Zig Ziglar recommends, enroll in "Automobile University." *(I'll expand on that later.)*

Perhaps you are thinking, ***"I do not have time to add one more program to my life."*** I felt exactly the same way when my supervisor suggested a seminar to me back in 1993. He didn't actually just suggest it; he required it. He had heard great reviews about an all-day "Success Seminar" that would be coming to Dallas and bought VIP tickets for the senior staff. These tickets entitled us to floor seats and a photo op with George Bush *(the forty-first president of the United States)*. **The featured speakers for the seminar included President Bush, General Norman Schwarzkopf, Dr. Robert**

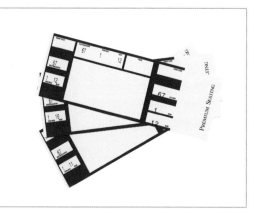

Schuller, one of my all-time heroes Zig Ziglar, Roger Staubach, and a man I wasn't familiar with named Peter Lowe.

Only fifty VIP seats were sold out of the 17,000 seats in the auditorium. Through a ticket glitch I ended up sitting on a folding chair added in front of the first row of the sold-out arena. To most folks that sounds pretty exciting, but I was in sales and would much rather sell all day than sit all day. But since the boss made arrangements and instructed us to appear at eight o'clock sharp, I had no other choice. So there I sat that morning, in front of the front row and right under the edge of the stage.

What a surprise awaited me at that seminar! Not only was I challenged and inspired, I returned to my office the next day more energized and motivated than I had ever been before. *I was ready to implement great new ideas, and I easily made up for what I had anticipated would be lost time.* But I had no idea what lasting and far-reaching effects that seminar would have on me.

PUTTING PROGRAMS INTO PRACTICE

Seven years later, my life as I had known it came to an abrupt halt. My high school sweetheart, the man I had married almost ten years earlier, chose to walk away, abandoning his entire life—including me. I went home that fateful day in July of 2000 to an eerily empty house. He was no longer there. The messages he left on answering machines at his work, for his family, and for me informed us that he was going in a new direction with his life. He promised that he would call once he got settled.

Months passed and that call never came. Extensive searches turned up no trace of him, and he was put on the National Missing Persons list. Over a year later authorities notified us that he had been found. The following day he called saying he wanted to "touch base." I knew from that conversation that he was never coming back. I had to obtain a divorce "by publication" in the newspaper.

Both the house and the mounting debt were awarded to me in the divorce. After settling our tangled financial affairs, I had to pick up the pieces of my life and start over again. What was I to do? Day after day I agonized and struggled over this question.

One day, in the midst of struggling to put my life back together, I remembered the seminar I attended years earlier. Out of all the success stories I heard that day, the one that stood out most was Peter

Lowe's. He recounted how he became the number one sales person at his company at the age of twenty-two, but that even with his success, something seemed to be missing in his life. One day he stopped and thought to himself, "There must be more to life than just this." And with that thought, he set out to find his calling. Peter Lowe secluded himself in a hotel room for three days. During that time he focused on making a list of the top twenty-five things he felt he was supposed to accomplish in his life. When he emerged from the hotel, he immediately put his plans into action. Success seminars topped his list. Today, Peter and Tamara Lowe's GET MOTIVATED! Seminar is well known as "America's #1 Business Seminar." The Lowes bring together noted speakers and leaders to inspire and motivate audiences in packed venues across the nation.

I applied Peter Lowe's process to my own situation. By focusing on my goals and aspirations, I found a new direction in my life. Within a few short months I began traveling down a new pathway, gaining much of what I had lost in previous years. While continuing to work and travel the nation speaking, I re-enrolled in college and completed the necessary 51 hours to receive my bachelor's degree—all in one calendar year. Talk about doing twice as much in half the time!

The university president even asked me to be the commencement speaker at my own graduation. I wasn't ready to stop there, and continued on to obtain my masters degree.

I moved far beyond my previous dreams and plans for my life simply *(but incredibly)* because I put into practice what I learned in an eight-hour program! You might be thinking that the addition of time-consuming programs **takes away** from your time. Initially, that might be true. But what you are actually doing is making **an investment** of your time. In my own life I was able to accomplish things that should have taken years in a matter of a just a few short months because of the knowledge I gained from a one-day investment. By adding programs to your life you, too, can learn to do things more efficiently in new, different, or better ways, thus allowing you to accomplish more in less time. The payoff will be seen in the future when the skills, strategies, and lessons learned will allow you to be a master manager of your time, thus allowing you to do twice as much in half the time; so make that investment, and then reap the benefits of the payoff! *This is the reason I passionately encourage you to add programs to your life. You never know when you might gain that small, invaluable nugget of information that will completely revolutionize your life.*

THE POWER OF PROGRAMS: PASS IT ON!

As part of Zig Ziglar's national speaking team I have observed the transformational power of programs many times. Several years ago, while working with the Army National Guard on behalf of Ziglar Training, I met a rookie recruiter with a very unusual last name. His fellow guardsmen called him Sgt. "I". Sgt. "I" was struggling to make mission (otherwise known to civilians as sales plan). Despite his best efforts, he struggled to get commitments. That was before attending a Ziglar Training program. At the program, Sgt. "I" heard the trainer say one thing that made all the difference in the world to his success as a recruiter.

The trainer talked about enrolling in **"Automobile University,"** something Mr. Ziglar taught for years. Simply put, one attends Automobile University by listening to educational material while driving in the car. A study by the University of Southern California has shown that if a person drives at least 12,000 miles a year *(as someone likely would in any metropolitan city),* and uses this method of education, in a matter of three years he or she would have the equivalency of two years of college education. What a bonus for commuters!

Sgt. "I" took Automobile University to heart. The training manual he received from Ziglar included seven CDs, so he started listening immediately. He listened to the CDs on the eight-hour commute from the seminar to his home office. When he finished the series, he started over again. The second time through, near the end of the CD entitled *Closes, Closes, Closes*, he heard something that revolutionized his closing process. Suddenly, Sgt. "I" knew he could do it! He stopped at a gas station about an hour from his destination, put on his uniform, and proceeded to the houses of two prospective Guardsmen he had been unable to sign.

He left both houses with recruitment documents from two newly-signed recruits. By spring of the following year, Sgt. "I" had made mission for the entire calendar year. At the end of that year he was honored as the number one National Guard recruiter in his state!

And to what did he attribute his success? It was all due to his "enrollment" in Automobile University!

What a difference one program can make! I write from personal experience. A program changed the course of my life, ultimately even leading me to become a featured speaker on "America's #1 Business Seminar." For the last six years I have been blessed with the opportunity to share my story from speaking platforms coast to coast, sharing the stage not only with Peter Lowe and Zig Ziglar (the man who launched my speaking career) but also with such notable speakers as Rudy Giuliani, Larry King, Dr. Robert Schuller, General Colin Powell, and Suze Orman. Looking back to when my life seemed to be falling apart, I could never have imagined where my life would be today.

ADD (+) PURPOSE:

Before we begin on this "Positive P" I have an important question for you. *Where are you going in your life?* To put it another way, **what is your purpose in life?** Have you ever stopped to consider the answer to that question? Often we become so involved in the "busy-ness" of life that we don't take the time to think about where we are going. If you want to learn how to do twice as much in half the time, the first thing you must determine is where you are going. For me it is essential to answer this question so that I use my hours, my days, my weeks, and so on, effectively.

Think about it this way: if I flew from Dallas to speak in Atlanta but did not know where I was going, what would I do when I exited the plane? I could rent a car and start driving. If I continued on this drive without any direction I could look really busy driving around, but I wouldn't go anywhere. Such aimless rambling would not make much sense, would it? Unfortunately, many people live their lives without direction. Now, let's change the scenario. This time I arrive in Atlanta with a destination in mind. I know where I am going, have clearly marked directions, and arrive at my destination in a timely fashion.

So I ask you, what is your destination? Where are you going and how do you plan to get there? In order to determine the answer, I challenge you to set aside this book *(but only temporarily!)* and contemplate exactly where you are going. Perhaps you, too, will want to use the method that Peter Lowe and many others have found to be so successful: list the top twenty-five things that you want to accomplish in your lifetime.

My personal Life List, such as the one produced by Peter Lowe, was created when I took time out from day-to-day activities, and spent time alone in prayer and deep thought to truly seek direction and meaning in my life. The result was a keen awareness of the pathway I must take. My list is the "key" that starts my engine and keeps me going! My journey is further fueled by the realization that the road ahead is not always easy, and that is alright! We must make allowances for some bumpy roads, detours, u-turns, wrong directions,

and even dead ends. Sometimes we even have to stop and create a new map in order to arrive at our destination. But one thing is certain: *having a purpose* will get you going in the right direction. **So good luck ... and enjoy the journey.**

ADD (+) PLANNING:

You have undoubtedly heard the phrase, *"Plan your work and work your plan."* Planning is as important as purpose because it gets you where you're going ... faster. To do twice as much in half the time, you can't approach your goals haphazardly. A well-thought plan will keep you clearly on track towards your goal; and the methods of planning are as varied as our personalities. So what is your method of planning?

I plan with lists. Back in my less-organized days I needed a list of my lists just to keep up with my lists! *(Perhaps some of you can relate to this dilemma.)* Now I work from only two planning lists: one for my day and one for my life. Each day I look at my "life list" posted on my bathroom mirror. It provides the big picture of where I want to steer my life. Then I look at how I will plan my day. Zig Ziglar says that if you spend just one percent of your day planning, you can spend the other 99% executing your plan. It works!

To plan my day, I simply get up fifteen minutes earlier than necessary and make my list for the day. Try setting your alarm fifteen minutes earlier than usual, and don't even think about snoozing through that buzzing! *(Remember that old saying, "You snooze ... you lose!")* Get right up and make your list, not only of what you **think** you can accomplish in a day, but everything you **need** to accomplish. Some of my "day lists" are short and some are long, depending on where I am with my current projects. But I always include at least one action step to take me toward those "big picture" goals in my life. The size of the action step does not matter; the main point is to do something each day that will take me closer to fulfilling my purpose in life.

You will be amazed at what you can accomplish once you take the time to plan. Don't be discouraged if something is still left on your list at the end of the day. You can always move it to the next day. With two lists in hand to guide you, let's see what comes next.

> *Our goals can only be reached through a vehicle of a plan,*
> *in which we must fervently believe, and upon which we*
> *must vigorously act. There is no other route to success.*
>
> Pablo Picasso

ADD (+) PRIORITIES:

Now it's time to prioritize. We start with a simple activity I learned from a Zig Ziglar *Time Management Training Course*. Make a list of activities that you engage in on a regular basis. Take some time to think this over so that the list will be as inclusive as possible. *(Some examples are reading, working, cleaning the house, going shopping, bike riding with your kids, etc.)* We will call these activities your "behaviors." Once you have completed your list, look back over these behaviors and think about why you do them.

√ *In other words, what value do they represent?*

Using the example from above, you might determine that you read to gain knowledge; therefore, gaining knowledge is the value. Look at work. Perhaps you do that for financial security. If so, financial security is the value that it represents. With riding bikes, the value is likely spending quality time with your family.

Next to each behavior you listed, briefly note why you value that activity/behavior. This exercise should provide insight into why you do the things you do.

Now make one additional list of your five most important values. *(Some examples are physical health, spiritual growth, family, and career.)* Prioritize the list by ranking these values one through five, starting with the value that is most important to you. Does your current schedule reflect your values? If not, it's time to re-prioritize so that you're spending time where it counts. Spending time on things that you don't value, or that are a low priority, isn't a good use of your precious time. Repeat this exercise periodically to help maintain your focus.

THE BIG ROCK

A common demonstration, called the *"big rock analogy,"* provides a strong visual example of the value of prioritizing. It goes like this: start with a large clear container, some pebbles, sand, and a large rock. Put the rock into the container first followed by the pebbles, which will fall all around it filling in the spaces. Then add enough sand so that the entire container is filled to the top. Everything fits perfectly. Then remove the contents of the container and change the order in which you fill it. If the sand goes in first, then the added contents will overflow from the top of the container. If the pebbles go in first, once again the added contents will overflow from the top of the

Got a
"BIG ROCK"
in your life?

Face it first.
*(So you don't get caught between
a rock and a hard spot!)*

Amy Jones

container. Those very same contents will be level with the top of the container only if the big rock goes in first! Now compare this graphic exercise with how you schedule your activities. Are you putting your *"big rocks"* in first, or are you changing the order and throwing your day out of balance, causing it to overflow? Let me share with you an awesome example of how an entire family changed as a result of establishing priorities. Previously, I related the story of how my life fell apart when the man I was married to completely abandoned his life. During that year when he could not be located, I felt alone and sad and at times, even afraid. I did not want anyone to know what happened. My situation was so confusing. I didn't understand it myself, so how could I possibly explain it to others? Besides that, I knew that he would want me to keep this private, so I worked very hard at maintaining a good façade.

That was until I met Kathy, a woman who worked in the payroll department at the company where I served as the director of public relations. Professionally Kathy and I had little interaction, and personally we had very little in common. Kathy was married and lived with her husband and four children in a small, well-kept house. Outside of the office, her life was solely dedicated to her husband, son, and three daughters. Their lives were filled with the children's sports and other family activities.

When Kathy began to reach out to me, after she noticed some changes in my personnel file, I realized just how different our lives were. Kathy would invite me to go to McDonald's with her family. She volunteered her husband to mow my yard and do handy-man work for me. Her entire family (kids included) moved my belongings from place to place as I tried to figure out where to stay. They always included me in family activities, and I always invited them to church. My church was an important constant in my life, and provided the much-needed stability during those difficult months. Kathy and her family were always too busy to go to church with me. They always said no to my invitation, but that didn't stop me from asking.

Although finances were tight, Kathy had plenty of love and fulfillment in her life. In fact, as far as I could see, Kathy had it all ... except for one thing. And it happened to be the one thing I had left, the one thing that kept me going through my awful nightmare. It was my faith. I thought about how Kathy was willing to share everything with me—her time, her family, her strength, her sense of humor, her dedication. What could I give her in return? What could I share with her? I had only one thing … and she didn't seem to need it.

Then came that fall day in 2001 when I received word that the man I had been married to was found. His phone call the next day made it clear he would never return. Relief swept over me upon learning he was physically alright; but after waiting in a state of limbo for so long, hoping he would return, the news was utterly devastating. Since Kathy was one of the few who knew what had been going on, I called her immediately. Sadness filled Kathy's voice, and I'll never forget what she said: "We'll do anything. What can we do to help you?" Selfishly, I responded, "Can you go to church with me tonight? Just tonight? I can't bear to go alone." For the first time, my invitation was not about them; it was about me. I could hear Kathy relaying the information to her husband Jim. He responded, "We'll go tonight … for Amy."

Suddenly my despair lifted and a wave of hope filled my heart. My spontaneous invitation had received a spontaneous response. I hadn't even planned it. *(That's just how God often works in our lives. That way, we can't take credit for the results!)* A few hours later they picked me up and we were on our way. Now what do you think this has to do with priorities? Just listen to the rest of the story.

That night at church, Kathy and her family found the one thing that was missing from their lives. That was seven years ago and they have rarely missed a weekend service since then. They all became

Christians and were baptized. In addition, Kathy and Jim teach a class for young married couples and serve as leaders for a small group, which meets in their home. Kathy is now employed in full-time ministry outside the church. The children participate in camps, mission trips, and many other activities. All six volunteer at church services. They are role models for Christ-centered living.

Their lives are still very busy. Even though the entire family is deeply involved with the church, they continue to be involved in family activities and the children's sports. But their "big rock" is their faith and commitment to their local church. That's the whole point of the story.

√ *Kathy and Jim got their priorities straight. They put the "big rock" in first and everything else fit!*

So remember ... once you complete your planning lists, you must go back and prioritize them. Ask yourself, *"What are the 'big rocks' going to be in my day, in my life?"* Then prioritize your lists accordingly. How do your two lists (day and life) fit together?

{ *Knowing what is most important in your life should guide you as you make decisions each day.* }

The strength of your character is rooted in the depth of your convictions.

Unknown

MULTIPLYING
Your Expectations

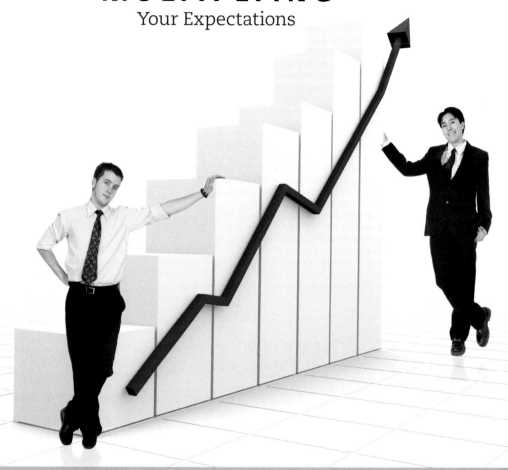

Now that we have subtracted and added, it's time to **multiply**. Even if you never liked multiplication, I guarantee you'll like it this way!

> *Here's how this part of the equation works:*
>
> ## MULTIPLY YOUR EXPECTATIONS OF YOURSELF, OF OTHERS, AND OF WHAT CAN BE DONE WITH YOUR TIME.

If you look at the answer to any multiplication problem, you will readily see that the number in the answer is much greater than the other numbers in the equation. It is the same with multiplying expectations. Putting this concept into action can lead to astonishing results. Let me tell you how it worked for me. *(And I **know** it can work for **you!**)*

Throughout my college years I developed and delivered drug prevention and anti-gang violence programs for elementary schools throughout Texas. *(Frequently I am still called upon to conduct these pro-*

grams in low socio-economic schools.) I look into the eyes of young people who have many expectations put upon them. Unfortunately these expectations are often negative. If society believes that these children are likely to become involved in drugs and violence, this belief can become a self-fulfilling prophecy. The encouraging news is that I have found many educators and administrators who truly feel a calling to teach these precious children. They hold the belief that these children can and will be successful, productive citizens who will contribute to society in a positive way. And with such positive expectations, amazing things can happen.

Back in the mid-nineties, I helped start Gen. Colin Powell's America's Promise Initiative in my home community. The local school district targeted 200 at-risk fifth graders and provided them with five fundamental resources specified by the America's Promise Program. A key element, and one of those

five resources, was to provide each child with an on-going relation-ship with a caring adult. One example of the success of this program is a child who went from failing grades to As and Bs in one semester.

What accounted for this change?

> *A caring adult looked into the eyes of that child and multiplied her expectations of him.*

Multiplied expectations work for grown-ups, too, as I discovered in my very first job. When I dropped out of college to get married, I landed what I thought was the greatest job in the world. I became the membership director of the only fine dining city club in Waco, Texas. I was young, naïve and full of enthusiasm. When I walked out of the elevator on the top floor of that bank building *(a skyscraper to me, yet only seven stories high!)* I immediately was drawn to the expan-sive windows and the impressive view they provided. I thought to myself, "I have arrived! Everyone in Waco is going to want a mem-bership in this club and I am going to help them get it!" Wow! I had never been into a city club before, and I could hardly wait to get started. What I did not know was that the club had been in a state of severe decline and had almost been closed down six months earlier.

I also did not know that the tax laws had changed and private club memberships had gone from being 100% deductible to zero deductibility, thus lessening the appeal of club membership.

I thought this was such a great place that I could sell it to anybody. A few months into my job, I found myself in a senior staff meeting.

At that time I had no idea what forecasting was, but in that meeting I quickly figured out that I was supposed to let the other department heads know how many memberships I thought I could sell by the end of that year. When it was my turn to speak, I boldly proclaimed that I would sell 500 memberships! The club manager looked at me, not believing what he had heard, and sarcastically remarked that if I could sell 500 memberships by the end of the year, he would throw a party for the staff in January and have a barber come and shave the number 500 on the back of his head. He thought he had a good laugh at my expense, but I responded by saying, *"You're on!"*

When the meeting was over I drew up a contract, had it notarized at the bank downstairs, asked each department head to sign it, and then plopped it down on the club manager's desk.

My actions surprised him, but he signed the contract anyway. Multiplied expectations ... WE WERE ON!

Without the aid of email and fax machines, I hand-delivered each membership packet and picked up any completed applications. I mounted a dry erase board on my office wall and wrote a big "500" in the middle of it. Each time a new member joined the club, I ran to my office, rang a bell, and slashed through the current number. By the end of summer, it became obvious to me that the other club employees started to expect a successful end to this challenge, and they acted accordingly. Banners soon appeared in the kitchen and other offices that said, "Club of the Year."

{
Everyone hoped this once-dying city club, now fully alive, might be recognized by the world's largest club company as the "Club of the Year." Could this possibly happen?

WELL, THAT BECAME THE MULTIPLIED EXPECTATION!
}

By early fall the club members got in on the action along with members of the community and even the Chamber of Commerce. As the year progressed I suddenly realized that the skeptical club manager expected it too!

On December 29th an unsuspecting prospect walked into the club and purchased the 500th membership! As of the last day of the year, we had not sold 499 memberships, and we had not sold 501 memberships. We had sold exactly 500! What could account for this incredible achievement? It could not be attributed to the talents or the experience of the people involved. It was the multiplied expectation. What a great lesson for everyone involved! It showed our club, as well as the entire community, that people can and do live up to multiplied expectations. Take my advice: if you multiply expectations, you will be amazed at what can be accomplished in a prescribed amount of time. We certainly were! Not only did we have a huge party to shave a "500" on the back of the club manager's head, but we were also named "Club of the Year." I was honored to be named "Membership Director of the Year" and highest ranking salesperson in the nation. All of this success came as a result of multiplying expectations. I am so grateful I learned this valuable lesson in my very first job. Using this concept has greatly enhanced my career and my life. Multiply your expectations of yourself and others and you will find yourself getting more done in less time.

Don't lower your expectations to meet your performance. Raise your level of performance to meet your expectations. Expect the best of yourself, and then do what is necessary to make it a reality.

Ralph Marston

DIVIDING
Give Yourself the Best Part

The word **TIME** *is composed of only four letters,* but if you divide the word you will see that there are two extremely important words inside. ***They are "I" and "Me."*** Extremely important words to all of us.

> *In order to make the best use of your time,*
> *in order to do twice as much in half the time,*
>
> ## YOU MUST TAKE TIME
> ## FOR "I" AND "ME."
>
> You must make time to recharge and be rejuvenated.

What is your "I and Me time?" What is the carrot you can dangle in front of your nose to get you through the work week, to the end of a project, or to motivate you to reach a goal? How do you reward yourself in such a way that you will be recharged and ready to go again? For some, it is a long weekend away with the family; for others it is something as simple as retreating to a quiet place with a good book. For me, my "I and Me time" is what wakes me up before 6:00 on Saturday morning. If I accomplished all I planned to do in the prior work week, then I can hardly wait for Saturday morning to arrive. I am up before the crack of dawn, dressed in a jogging suit ... no make-up ... my hair in a pony tail. Where do you think I am headed? To the gym? To the jogging trail? No! I am running out the door to go to garage sales! I told you I like "stuff," and garage sales are the very best places to find it! But since I am now a "recovering stuff-a-holic," I garage sale to benefit other people in my life.

I have lists of the wants and needs and sizes of all my family and friends so that I can make "buy of a lifetime" purchases for them.

My "I and Me time" is quite rewarding for two different reasons. First, I love to find and buy "stuff," and secondly I love to give "stuff" away. Once I finish shopping, I start delivering. That keeps me from having to "subtract" when I get home!

Several years ago my younger brother lived in Chicago while working on his PhD. His wife was a stay-at-home mom so finances were extremely tight. As you might expect, my brother's wardrobe was quite lacking and he would not spend money on clothes for himself. One lucky Saturday I hit upon a garage sale in a very upscale neighborhood where a man, who had just moved to Texas from Chicago and happened to be my brother's size, was selling his entire winter wardrobe. Top designer-labeled shirts under cleaner bags, barely worn pants and jeans, like-new jackets and sweaters! Talk about getting recharged! I hit the jackpot! That afternoon I shipped my brother's "new wardrobe" to him. I am fairly certain that many of you would not choose garage sales for your "I and Me time." What will your choice be?

I challenge you to plan some "I and Me time" into your calendar, just for you and you alone. But it is very important to remember this: your "I and Me time" should not be what's left over in your day or week. It must be included in your plans ahead of time.

 You don't want your "I and Me time" to end up as the remainder in your division equation!

The Great EQUAL-izer

Balancing It All Out

What do all equations have in common? An equal sign.
In a mathematical equation the equal sign represents the balance;
and in our equation of effective life/time management,
it *represents balance.*

{
DO YOU HAVE AN EQUAL SIGN IN YOUR LIFE?
What is your balance?
}

As I shared previously, when my life fell apart my faith, family, friends and foundation kept me grounded and balanced.

Look around you and you will see people who go and go and go all day every day; but if they have no balance, sooner or later their lives will crash around them. **Balance is essential to a happy, productive, well-lived life.** My friend and mentor, Zig Ziglar, taught me a lot about balance. *(He is probably the most balanced person I know.)* So, with his permission, I would like to share a tool he uses to help people determine if they have balance.

Zig looks at balance in terms of a wheel that he calls the Wheel of Life. To illustrate this concept, first, draw a large circle. Then draw spokes from the center of the circle to the outer edge. Make one spoke for each important area in your life: Personal, Family, Business, Mental, Physical, Spiritual, and Financial. Label each spoke and then write the numbers one through ten down the side of each spoke (starting at the center with number one and ending with the number ten on the outer edge). On each of the spokes, make a dot where you think you are right now in your life, with one representing the need for improvement and ten representing the ultimate or pinnacle of success. Be as honest as possible, and be careful not to take the easy way out—the middle road so to speak—by plotting yourself at a five or six on each one.

Now connect all the dots to create your own Wheel of Life. *What if you were to take this wheel, along with three more identical ones, and put them on a vehicle?* How bumpy would your ride be? Most people discover that their wheel is not as big and round as they expected. What would it take to give you a smoother ride? You would need bigger and rounder wheels!

Let's make this example analogous to traveling down the road of life. To avoid a "bumpy ride," you need to balance the things that are most important. Look at your wheel and determine the areas where you need to refocus your time.

NOW, BALANCE THOSE WHEELS AND GET MOVING!

Problems arise in that one has to find a balance between what people need from you and what you need for yourself.

Jessye Norman

Make Your Time Count!

Now that you know how to solve the equation for successful life/time management, let's go back to another basic in mathematics ... the very foundation. What was the very first thing you learned in math, even before adding? **It was counting!**

> *If you take away only one piece of advice from this book, I hope it is this:*
> **MAKE YOUR TIME COUNT!**

I learned first hand about making time count nine years ago when my seemingly healthy 55 year-old father, in the prime of his life and career, was diagnosed with stage four terminal kidney cancer. Suddenly he was faced with not knowing how much time he had left on this earth. That was almost as devastating to my dad as the diagnosis. All of his life he had been an efficient, hard-working, dedicated man who rose to the top of corporate America by managing his time well and teaching others to do the same. He was vice-president of a Fortune 500 company, and long-range planning was one of his specialties.

Three days after his diagnosis he called a family meeting at our home. This had been our family's usual method of addressing problems when I was growing up. As my entire family sat together in a circle on the floor, he explained his condition to us and shared that he had hardly slept at all during the three previous nights because he so desperately wanted to know how much time he had left. These thoughts totally consumed him. It was as if he was more worried about the length of time that he had left than battling terminal cancer. He looked haggard as he spoke to us. He told us that around 3:00 that morning, while lying on his bed completely exhausted, he simply cried out to God, "How much time?"

What my dad said next was not only astonishing, but it also changed my entire outlook on life and time. He got his answer. It was only one word. It didn't come in a booming voice. It was not even audible. But when he cried out with his deepest conviction, the answer came: "Enough." That was it—enough time to do everything that he was put on this earth to accomplish. My dad slept peacefully the rest of the morning and awoke with more dedication and determination than I had ever seen before. He did more to make time count in the following six months than at any time in his entire 55 years. And besides that, he no longer had to worry about "how long?" because whatever the length, he knew it would be enough.

The question that concerned my dad faces all of us. The reality is that none of us knows the answer. But we can be sure of this:

> *If we make each and every moment count,*
> *we will have* ***"ENOUGH"*** *time.*

Have the Time of Your Life

I challenge you today to start making your time count. Begin by:

Subtracting $(-)$ Subtracting the "stuff" *(both physical and mental)* that steals your time.

Adding $(+)$ Add back the positives: programs, purpose, planning and priorities.

Multiplying (X) Achieve astonishing results by multiplying your expectations of yourself and others.

Dividing $(/)$ Divide the word "time" to remind yourself of the all-important "I and Me time."

Equals $(=)$ Don't forget that balance equals a smoother ride.

Finally, when you get to the end of the day, look back and count again. This time, count your many blessings. You have been given 86,400 seconds … that's 24 hours each and every day.
What an incredible gift of time each of us has been given!

HOW WILL YOU MAKE IT COUNT?

Acknowledgments

Peter and Tamara Lowe … who would have known that what I learned from you sitting in one of your seminars many years ago would one day so profoundly affect the course of my life? I will be forever grateful! Thank you for your bold faith, for helping me realize that God really did have a plan for my life, and for your willingness to share your success with others.

Dr. Gary and Mrs. Sheila Cook … you are truly my "extended family," the one that God provided when I needed it the most. You have faithfully offered listening ears and sound advice. Thank you for showing me by your example the meaning of servant leadership. *(And just knowing that you are "in my corner" means so much to me!)*

Ebby Halliday Acers … what an inspiration you are, Ebby! You are my role model for strength, determination, perseverance, and dedicated community service. *(Besides that, you are so much fun!)* If I am still "going strong" like you are at age 98, I will say it is because I had a good friend named Ebby Halliday Acers! You are a true hero to me!

Zig Ziglar ... you not only launched my speaking career, but you helped launch a new and wonderful phase in my life. I am deeply indebted to you and your wife Jean for your inspiration, encouragement, and guidance, but most of all for your friendship. This book is a reality because you encouraged me to write it and taught me how to turn my spoken words into written words. What an inspiration you have been! Thank you for being such an outstanding example of a man of faith and integrity.

Mac Anderson, Lynn Harker, Stephanie Trannel and all the folks at Simple Truths ... you took a look at my writing ... and saw a book! Then you stuck with me through edits, emails, phone conversations, and rewrites until it was completed. Thanks for giving me the privilege of being one of your authors. I'm in such great company!

My friends and family ... thank you for your continuing love and support and for sharing your own "gifts of time" with me.

About the Author

There is a saying that goes, "If you want to get something done, ask a busy person." Few people personify this statement better than Amy Jones. Her high-energy "busy-ness" propelled her to the forefront of the business world. At the age of twenty-three, she ranked #1 in membership sales throughout the nation, working for the largest private club company in the world. With a speaking career launched by her friend and mentor, Zig Ziglar, she has traveled the nation taking her message of "How To Do Twice As Much In Half The Time" to hundreds of thousands of people. She is a dynamic and engaging corporate speaker who motivates and inspires, sharing from her expertise in the areas of sales, communication, leadership, and time management. Amy, who is a speaker/

trainer for Ziglar, Inc. and is a co-founder and the Executive Director of the "Journey of Sisters" ministry, holds a Master of Arts degree in Professional Development with a concentration in Leadership Studies. While many would agree that Amy has proven her skills in the business world, her real motivation is the "busy-ness" of making a positive difference in the lives of others. This is truly a gift ... to herself and to all whose lives she touches.

For more information, please visit
www.twiceasmuchinhalfthetime.com

simple truths®
THE GIFT OF INSPIRATION

THE SIMPLE TRUTHS DIFFERENCE

I f you have enjoyed this book we invite you to check out our entire collection of gift books, with free inspirational movies, at **www.simpletruths.com.**

You'll discover it's a great way to inspire *friends* and *family,* or to thank your best *customers* and *employees.*

Our products are *not available in bookstores ... only direct.* Therefore, when you purchase a gift from Simple Truths you're giving something that can't be found elsewhere!

For more information, please visit us at:

www.simpletruths.com

Or call us toll free…

800-900-3427